Omelet Breakfast

The Best Omelet Recipes from Around the World

BY

Daniel Humphreys

License Notes

Table of Contents

Introduction

For many families, making omelets have become part of their breakfast routine. What many don't understand is that omelets recipes can be tweaked to deliver healthy snacks and fulfilling dinners. This is no surprise, given that fact that many people around the world have been made to believe omelets are meant for breakfasts only.

Now, there are a million ways to twist the omelet recipe you know to make a different satisfying meal. However, to do this successfully, you must comprehend all Omelet recipe basics. Grasping the basics will help you get your choice of ingredients right as well as their proportions based on the size of omelet you want to make. But first, do you know what an omelet is?

What is an omelet?

What comes to your mind when an omelet is mentioned? Eggs? To put it simply, an omelet is a dish that is made from eggs, fried without stirring. The dish can be served plain or topped with other ingredients such as mushroom, cheese, minced meat, and chives. It's difficult to trace the origin of this dish, but its emergence is credited to both the Romans and French.

Since its inception in the 16th century, the meal has metamorphosed into different meals that delight people across the globe regardless of the culture or cuisine. There are numerous versions of this meal, each bearing a different name. For instance, the omelet is the Greek name for an omelet, frittata in Italia, nergesi in Iran, Khai jiao in Thailand, tamagoyaki in Japan, and many more. All these terms refer to one dish, but there are vivid variations with regard to the ingredients used, hence the final taste.

Most Popular Omelet Ingredients

Omelet has so many variations and ranks as one of the best meals for breakfast. Each cuisine has its own version of the omelet. The variation is primarily because of the type of ingredients used. Here are the main ingredients used to make an omelet:

- Eggs
- Mushroom
- Ham
- Tomato
- Cheese
- Chorizo
- Sausage
- Green pepper
- Spinach
- Scallions
- Avocado
- Bacon
- Tofu
- Salsa
- Broccoli
- Cream
- Shredded potato

- Steak
- Garlic

Health Benefits Of Eating Omelets

The reason why omelets are very popular is that they are not only delicious but also packs a punch in terms of their health benefits. Here are some of the salient benefits of eating omelets:

- They are rich in protein
- They prevent cravings
- Support brain health
- Maintains a good nerve system
- They a rich in vitamins
- They are a good source of energy
- Maintain healthy blood circulation
- Increase immunity

If you are bored by taking one omelet dish every morning, perhaps the recipes below will give you a reason to smile.

Ham and Feta Omelet

This is a delicious easy to make feta omelet, piled with tomatoes, onions, and oregano, making it nutritious and awesome to kick off your day with. This omelet can be carried in your lunchbox or as a snack.

Time: 20 Minutes

Serving: 2

Ingredients

- 1 green onion (chopped)
- 1 tbsp milk
- 4 eggs
- tbsp basil (dried)
- tbsp oregano (dried)
- Garlic powder (dash)
- Salt
- Pepper
- 1 tbsp butter
- Cup feta cheese (crumbled)
- 3 slices ham (chopped)
- 1 plum tomato (chopped)
- 2 tbsp balsamic vinaigrette

Method

1. Whisk together onions, milk, eggs, and seasonings in a mixing bowl. Melt butter in your non-stick skillet over medium heat then pour the mixture.

2. As the mixture cooks, push the cooked parts to the center letting the uncooked portion flow underneath.

3. When all the eggs are cooked then place ham and cheese on one side then fold the omelet to cover the ham and cheese.

4. Cut into half and serve with tomatoes.

5. Drizzle balsamic vinaigrette

Nutritional Information

- Cal: 289
- Fat: 20g
- Carbs: 5g
- Fiber: 1g
- Protein: 21g
- Sugar: 3g

Basic French Omelet

This omelet is a versatile and a classic recipe to prepare. It is a healthy recipe with plenty of eggs. Eggs are rich in lutein and zeaxanthin antioxidants which are essential for eye health.

Time: 7 Minutes

Servings: 1

Ingredients

- 2 eggs (beaten)
- 2 tbsp water
- tbsp salt
- Dash pepper
- 1 tbsp butter
- Cup shredded cheese

Method

1. Combine the eggs, salt, pepper, and water in a mixing bowl until blended completely.

2. Over medium heat, heat butter in a skillet until hot; tilting the pan to coat the bottom.

3. Pour in the mixture. The edges will set immediately.

4. Push the cooked parts gently from the edges to center for uncooked portions to flow underneath and reach the hot surface of the pan.

5. Continue to cook while tilting the pan and moving cooked portions gently as needed.

6. When no liquid egg is visible, and the top surface is thickened, top the omelet with shredded cheese on one side and fold the omelet into half using the inverted turner.

7. Enjoy warm.

Nutritional Information

- Calories: 177
- Fat: 13g
- Sodium: 434mg
- Carbs: 1g
- Fiber: 0g
- Protein: 13g
- Calcium: 58.8mg
- Iron: 1.8mg

Mediterranean Omelet

This is a fluffy, quick, and satisfying Mediterranean flavored omelet that leaves your taste buds thanking you and wanting more. The Mediterranean **Ingredients** in this recipe make it unique and definitely worth trying.

Time: 15 Minutes

Serving: 1

Ingredients

- 2 eggs
- Oregano
- 1 tbsp milk
- Salt and pepper to taste
- 1 tbsp butter or oil
- 2 tbsp tomato (diced)
- 2 tbsp kalamata olives (sliced)
- 1 artichoke heart (quartered)
- 1 tbsp feta (crumbled)
- 1 tbsp romesco sauce

Method

1. Mix egg, oregano, milk, salt and pepper in a mixing bowl.

2. Heat oil in a non-stick skillet then pour the mixture to cover the skillet bottom.

3. When the eggs are almost set, sprinkle the diced tomato, kalamata olives, artichoke hearts, and the crumbled feta on half of the egg then fold the other half over.

4. Continue cooking for a minute then remove from skillet. Top with romesco sauce then enjoy.

Nutritional Information

- Cal: 303
- Fat: 17.7g
- Carbs: 21.9g
- Fiber: 9.9g
- Protein: 18.2g
- Sugar: 4.4g

Kedgeree Omelet

This is an easy, delicious and a classic omelet dish. Kedgeree is a dish of rice (curried), smoked fish, flaked and eggs (boiled hard). The kedgeree is wrapped in an omelet to make a hearty meal perfect for lunch or dinner.

Time: 25 Minutes

Servings: 2

Ingredients

- Haddock fillet, smoked (about 250g)
- 400ml milk
- 1 diced onion
- Sunflower oil
- 1 tbsp
- Turmeric
- 100g peas (frozen)
- 2 tbsp korma curry paste
- Pouch pilau rice, cooked
- 4 eggs
- 2 tbsp flat-leaf parsley (chopped)
- Mango chutney to serve

Method

1. Put milk in a pan over high heat and place the fish making sure it is completely covered by the milk. Place the lid and bring to simmer or until the milk starts to bubble. Turn off heat and let the fish rest for about 5 Minuteswhile covered.

2. Put 1 tbsp oil in a skillet, add onion and fry until soft. Add turmeric, korma paste, peas and rice then cook for about 5 minutes. In the meantime, remove fish from milk and remove bones and skin. Flake the fish into chunks and stir it in the rice mix.

3. Whisk 2 eggs at ago with 1 tbsp parsley and season. Heat 1tsp oil in another pan and fry the eggs making a thin omelet. Repeat for the other two eggs.

4. Divide the kedgeree among the two omelets and fold.

5. Serve and enjoy.

Nutritional Information

- Calories: 618
- Protein: 49.1g
- Saturates: 9.3g

Bacon Spinach Omelet

Want to feel like in a five-star restaurant taking a hearty breakfast right at your home? This is a perfect omelet recipe just for you. It's wonderful and easy to make, rich in nutrition making your morning brilliant.

Time: 10 Minutes

Serving: 1

Ingredients

- 4 slices bacon
- 4 eggs (beaten)
- 3 tbsp milk or half/half
- Salt and pepper
- Cup cherry tomatoes (sliced)
- Cup spinach (chopped)
- 0.5 cup cheese (grated)

Method

1. Preheat your oven to 4500 F.

2. Cut bacon into small pieces and cook in a pan to the desired crispness. Remove cooked bacon from the pan.

3. Combine milk with the beaten eggs in a mixing bowl, then add salt and pepper. Stir to combine.

4. Heat the pan with grease then cook the mixture until the eggs' bottom is well cooked.

5. Add tomatoes, spinach, cheese, and the cooked bacon.

6. Transfer to the oven and cook for about two minutes.

7. Remove from the oven and close the sides over. You may add toppings of your choice.

8. Enjoy warm.

Nutritional Information

- Cal: 883
- Fat: 71g
- Carbs: 7g
- Protein: 49g
- Sugar: 4g

Courgette Souffle Omelet

This is an easy-to-make, delicious courgette soufflé omelet dish. It takes 30 Minutesto prepare this meal, making it a perfect mid-week meal for the bachelors.

Time: 25 Minutes

Servings: 1

Ingredients

- Butter
- 1 grated courgette, medium
- 2 finely chopped spring onions
- Olive oil
- 2 eggs (separated)
- 1 tbsp grated parmesan
- Green salad to serve

Method

1. Heat butter in a pan then add onion and courgette. Cook until courgette become soft and all water is evaporated. Season and remove from the pan.

2. Whisk egg yolks in a medium bowl with water and season. Whisk egg whites in another bowl until soft peaks form. Mix the egg whites and egg yolks retaining as much air as you can.

3. Add butter to the nonstick pan. Add the eggs mixture and gently cook until bottom is set. Add the cooked courgette.

4. Sprinkle parmesan and fold over. Cook for another few Minutesuntil top is set.

5. Top with green salad and enjoy.

Nutritional Information

- Calories: 350
- Fat: 27.6g
- Carbs: 3.3g
- Fiber: 2.2g
- Protein: 21.1g

Baked Omelet Squares

These are very delicious and easy to make Christmas morning omelet squares. Can also be accompanied by sausage balls to make an awesome Christmas brunch. This omelet squares recipe is worth a trial.

Time: 45 Minutes

Serving: 8

Ingredients

- Cup butter
- 1 onion (chopped)
- Cup cheddar cheese (shredded)
- 1 can mushrooms (sliced)
- 1 can black olives (sliced)
- Ham (chopped and cooked) optional
- Jalapeno peppers (sliced) optional
- 12 eggs (scrambled)
- Cup milk
- tbsp salt and pepper

Method

1. Preheat your oven to 4000 F, then grease a medium baking dish

2. Over medium-high heat, melt butter in a non-stick skillet. Fry onions to the desired tenderness.

3. Evenly spread cheese on the baking dish, then layer sliced mushrooms, sliced olives, onions, chopped ham, and sliced jalapeno peppers.

4. In a mixing bowl mix eggs and milk, then season with pepper and salt to taste. Pour the mixture on the baking dish.

5. Bake in the oven, uncovered until the top is slightly brown and center is not runny.

6. Let cool before cutting into squares and servings.

Nutritional Information

- Cal: 344
- Fat: 27.3g
- Carbs: 7.2g
- Fiber: 2g
- Protein: 17.9g
- Sugar: 4g

Crab, Chilli And Herb Omelet

This omelet is gluten-free, rich in protein and low in calorie. It is one of the easiest recipes to prepare and a perfect one for midweek meals. It is a super healthy recipe since crab contains Riboflavin which is vital for the production of red blood cells and steroids which are good in promoting normal growth.

Time: 20 Minutes

Servings: 1

Ingredients

- 100g white crab meat
- 1 diced red chili
- 1 tbsp chopped coriander
- 1 tbsp chopped dill
- 1 tbsp chopped chives
- 1 tbsp low-fat crème Fraiche
- 2 eggs (beaten until pale)
- Olive oil
- Leaf salad and herb to serve

Method

1. Mix chili, coriander, dill, chives, crab and crème Fraiche then season well.

2. Heat 1tsp olive oil in a pan. Meanwhile, season the egg mixture with salt.

3. Pour the eggs mixture into the pan and fry to make a thin omelet.

4. Put the crab mixture on top and fold the omelet in half. Warm through for about 1 minute.

5. Serve the omelet with leaf salad and herb.

Nutritional Information

- Calories: 297
- Fat: 16.9g
- Carbs: 1.7g
- Sugar: 1.3g
- Fiber: 0.3g
- Protein: 34.3g
- Salt: 1.2g

Egg White and Corn Omelet

This corn omelet is creamy, sweet and very easy to prepare. Try this omelet at your home for breakfast to kick off the day in high spirits and to keep yourself and your family members full until the next meal.

Time: 10 Minutes

Servings: 2

Ingredients

- 8 egg whites
- Cup creamed corn
- Pepper
- 20g butter
- Sour cream
- Dill sprigs (fresh)

Method

1. In a small mixing bowl, combine the egg whites with creamed corn. Season with pepper to taste.

2. Preheat your grill on medium heat. Then over medium heat, melt 10g butter in a frying pan. Pour half of the mixture to cover the pan base and let it cook until the egg is set.

3. Place the pan under the preheated grill to grill until the omelet is slightly browned.

4. Now your omelet is ready! Slide it onto a serving plate then cover. Repeat the process with all the mixture is used up.

5. Top with cream and fresh dill then enjoy.

Nutritional Information

- Cal: 950
- Fat: 12.7g
- Carbs: 11.8g
- Fiber: 2.3g
- Protein: 15.6g

Smoked Trout and Gruyere Omelet

This is a quick and easy omelet recipe to have for a mid-week meal. This recipe is healthy as the sodium minerals that are contained in gruyere helps to maintain the balance of fluid in the body.

Time: 20 Minutes

Servings: 2

Ingredients

- Butter
- 2 sliced spring onions
- 4 eggs (beaten)
- 120g hot-smoked trout (cut into chunks)
- 4 tbsp four-cheese sauce (ready-made)
- 15g gruyere (finely-grated)
- 1 tbsp chopped chives
- Rocket dressing to serve

Method

1. Place a non-stick pan on a hot grill then melt butter. Add onions and sauté for about 4 minutes.

2. Add eggs and make a thin omelet. Cook, drawing in the sides to let uncooked egg flow underneath.

3. Once the top is set, add trout then top with sauce to cover the tout completely.

4. Sprinkle the cheese on top and grill until bubbles form on top and omelet is golden.

5. Sprinkle over chives and top with rocket dressing.

6. Enjoy warm.

Nutritional Information

- Calories: 303
- Fat: 19.4g
- Carbs: 2.6g
- Sugar: 0.9g
- Fiber: 0.9g
- Protein: 29g
- Salt: 1.9g

Baby Spinach Omelet

This is a perfect breakfast omelet to kick off your day. It's easy to prepare and keeps you full for a long time. The baby spinach and cheese bring out a hearty taste, making your taste buds yearn for more.

Time: 15 Minutes

Serving: 1

Ingredients

- 2 eggs
- tbsp parmesan cheese Grated)
- 1 cup torn baby spinach
- tbsp nutmeg (ground)
- tbsp onion powder
- Salt and pepper

Method

1. Beat eggs in a mixing bowl then stir in cheese and baby spinach. Add ground nutmeg onion powder, salt, and pepper for seasoning.

2. Spray your non-stick skillet with cooking spray then heat over medium heat. Pour the egg mixture and cook until the egg is partially set. Flip to cook on the other side to your desired doneness.

3. Enjoy.

Nutritional Information

- Cal: 186
- Fat: 12.3g
- Carbs: 2.8g
- Fiber: 0.8g
- Protein: 16.4g
- Sugar: 1g

Slow Cooker Veggie Omelet

This omelet is purely simple since everything is put in a slow cooker and after 2 hours it's ready. It's a delicious and a super-healthy slow-cooker breakfast to prepare.

Time: 2 Hours 10 Minutes

Servings: 4

Ingredients

- 6 eggs
- Cup milk
- tbsp salt
- Ground pepper (fresh) to taste
- tbsp garlic powder
- tbsp chili powder
- 1 cup broccoli florets
- 1 thinly-sliced bell pepper
- 1 finely-chopped yellow onion
- 1 minced garlic clove

Garnish

- Cheddar cheese, shredded
- Chopped tomatoes
- Parsley (fresh)

Method

1. Grease the inside of your slow cooker lightly with the cooking spray and set aside.

2. Mix eggs, salt, garlic powder, pepper, milk and chili powder in a mixing bowl and use an egg beater to whisk thoroughly until combined well.

3. Place sliced peppers, onions, broccoli florets and garlic in a slow cooker. Add the egg mixture and stir.

4. Cover and cook on high settings for about 2 hours. Check at 1 hour 30 Minutesfor the first time. If the eggs are set then the omelet is done.

5. Sprinkle the cheese on top and cook for about 3 Minuteswhile covered for the cheese to melt.

6. Turn off slow cooker then cut the omelet to 8 wedges

7. Garnish with parsley, onions, and onions

8. Serve and enjoy!

Nutritional Information

- Calories: 142
- Fat: 7g
- Sodium: 263mg
- Potassium: 306mg
- Carbs: 8g
- Protein: 10g

Baked Omelet

Looking for a delicious, simple to make breakfast, a brunch dish or a Christmas breakfast for your family or visitors? Then this baked omelet is the one for you. It's full of nutrients and quite filling.

Time: 55 Minutes

Serving: 4

Ingredients

- 1 cup milk
- 8 eggs (beaten)
- tbsp salt
- 3oz ham (diced and cooked)
- Cup cheddar cheese (shredded)
- Cup mozzarella cheese (shredded)
- 1 tbsp onion (dried and minced)

Method

1. Preheat your oven to 3500 F.

2. Grease your casserole dish and set it aside.

3. Mix milk and eggs. Stir in salt, diced ham, shredded cheese (cheddar and mozzarella) and onion.

4. Pour the mixture into the greased casserole dish then bake uncovered for 45 minutes.

Nutritional Information

- Cal: 314
- Fat: 9.0g
- Carbs: 5.9g
- Fiber: 0.1g
- Protein: 24.8g
- Sugar: 4g

Baked Ham and Cheese Omelet

This baked ham and cheese omelet only requires 5 Minutesto prepare. It is a healthy breakfast recipe with amazing flavors and is also incredibly versatile. Your family will absolutely love it.

Time: 50 Minutes|

Servings: 6

Ingredients

- 8 eggs (beaten)
- 1 cup milk
- tbsp salt (seasoned)
- 8 Ounces cooked ham (diced)
- 1 Cup shredded cheddar cheese
- 3 tbsp chopped onions
- Fresh chives

Method

1. In a medium mixing bowl, mix the eggs with milk. Season with salt and stir thoroughly.

2. Add ham, onion, and cheese, then stir to combine.

3. Pour the egg mixture to a greased baking dish.

4. Bake for about 45 Minutesat 3500 F until eggs are well cooked, and the omelet is set

5. Cut to squares then garnish with chives.

6. Serve.

Nutritional Information

- Calories: 278
- Fat: 19g
- Sodium: 860mg
- Potassium: 268mg
- Carbs: 3g
- Protein: 21g

Oven Denver Omelet

This is an awesome, fluffy, light breakfast omelet that can be prepared ahead of time in those busy mornings. It's packed with cheese, ham, and pepper giving it a glamorous taste.

Time: 40 Minutes

Servings: 8

Ingredients

- 0.5 cup half and half
- 8 eggs
- 1 cup ham (finely chopped and cooked)
- 1 cup cheddar cheese (shredded)
- Cup green pepper (minced)
- Cup onion (minced)
- tbsp parsley (optional)

Method

1. Preheat your oven to 4000F then grease a medium baking dish.

2. Beat half and half and eggs until fluffy.

3. Stir in cheddar cheese, cooked ham, pepper, minced onion, and parsley.

4. Pour the mixture into the baking dish and bake until the egg is set.

5. Enjoy.

Nutritional Information

- Cal: 262.8
- Fat: 18.9g
- Carbs: 2.5g
- Fiber: 0.2g
- Protein: 19.8g
- Sugar: 0.8g

2 Minute Egg Omelet In A Mug

This is a healthy breakfast recipe which only takes a few Minutesto prepare. This egg omelet is delicious, and everyone in your family will love its custom flavors. It is the best recipe for someone looking to cut down fat, calories and cholesterol.

Time: 2 Minutes

Servings: 1

Ingredients

- Cooking spray
- 2 eggs
- 1 tbsp diced roasted red peppers
- Cup spinach
- 1 tbsp feta cheese
- 1 tbsp sliced green onions
- Pepper to taste

Method

1. Add the eggs in a small mixing bowl, then using a fork beat until yokes and the white combines.

2. Add red pepper, feta cheese, spinach, green onions, and the pepper to taste then stir.

3. Pour the mixture into a microwave dish. Place the dish in the microwave and cook for about 1.5 minutes. Remove the omelet from microwave and let sit for about 1 minute.

4. Serve

Nutritional Information

- Calories: 187
- Sugar: 2g
- Sodium: 317mg
- Fat: 13g
- Carbs: 3g
- Protein: 14g
- Cholesterol: 431mg

Old Widow Walker's Ziploc Omelets

This is an awesomely simple delicious Ziploc omelet that is full of nutrients, and that can be taken for breakfast or carried to work as a snack. Preparing this omelet can be a family activity since it is easy to make.

Time: 33 Minutes

Servings: 5

Ingredients

- 10 eggs
- 2 cups cheese (grated)
- 1 cup ham (chopped)
- 1 cup bacon (crumbled)
- Green pepper
- Onion
- 1 cup tomatoes (chopped)
- 1 cup hash brown (thawed)

Method

1. Crack two eggs in each of the five Ziploc freezer bags. Shake well to combine.

2. Add cheese, chopped ham, crumbled bacon, pepper, onion, chopped tomatoes, and hash browns in each bag.

3. Zip up the bags ensuring there is no air inside then put the zipped bags in boiling water for thirteen minutes.

4. Remove the bags from water, unzip them, and roll out the omelets.

5. Server and enjoy.

Nutritional Information

- Cal: 269
- Fat: 39.1g
- Carbs: 17g
- Fiber: 1.4g
- Protein: 32.3g
- Sugar: 1.8g

Zucchini, Onion and Feta Cheese Omelet

This is a perfect vegetarian omelet recipe ready in 20 minutes. It is a healthy dinner dish since zucchini contains zeaxanthin and lutein which help maintain and improve eye health.

Time: 20 Minutes

Servings: 2

Ingredients

- tbsp olive oil
- Cup chopped onion
- Cup grated zucchini
- 3 eggs
- 2 egg whites
- 3 tbsp water
- tbsp salt
- tbsp ground pepper
- 1 tbsp crumbled feta cheese
- 2 tbsp flat-leaf parsley (minced)

Method

1. Put olive oil in a skillet and heat over medium heat.

2. Add onion and cook for about 4 Minuteswhile occasionally stirring until the onions begin to turn brown.

3. Add zucchini and cook for another 2 minutes, then transfer to a plate and cover with aluminum foil to retain the warmth.

4. Meanwhile, whisk the eggs, egg whites and water in a bowl until combined well.

5. Wipe the skillet then spay with the cooking spray. Increase to medium-high heat.

6. Add the egg mixture to the skillet and cook until edges start to set. Lift the omelet edges gently with a spatula tilting the pan to allow the liquid egg flow to the pan bottom. Do this continually as the omelet is cooking.

7. Cook the omelet until center is set then season with pepper and salt.

8. Place the vegetable mixture on top of half omelet and top with feta cheese. Fold the omelet.

9. Cut into half then garnish with parsley and serve.

Nutritional Information

- Calories: 160
- Fat: 10g
- Cholesterol: 247mg
- Sodium: 430mg
- Carbs: 5g
- Fiber: 1g
- Sugars: 3g
- Protein: 13g

Apple Bacon and Cheese Omelet

This is an awesomely delicious breakfast omelet with apples bringing out a sweet flavor and a textured touch which helps kick off your day in high spirits. This omelet is quite healthy and keeps you full until the next meal.

Time: 25 Minutes

Serving: 2

Ingredients

- 3 tbsp butter (unsalted)
- Sweet apple (peeled and thinly sliced)
- 6 eggs
- 4 tbsp whole milk
- tbsp salt
- tbsp black pepper (freshly ground)
- 2 tbsp blue cheese (crumbled)
- 2 slices bacon (cooked and crumbled)

Method

1. Over medium heat, melt 1 tbsp of butter in a non-stick skillet. Add sweet apples and stir cook until softened.

2. Remove the skillet from heat and transfer the apples to a heatproof bowl. Set the apples aside. Use a paper towel to wipe out the remaining butter from the skillet.

3. Mix eggs, whole milk, salt, and black pepper in a mixing bowl until well combined.

4. Return the skillet on heat and melt 1 tbsp of butter until well heated. Pour half of the mixture onto the skillet. Stir cook until small curds are formed.

5. Shake the skillet gently to spread the mixture evenly on the skillet.

6. Sprinkle half the cheese, half the cooked apples and half the cooked bacon at the middle third of the cooking egg mixture.

7. Remove the skillet from heat and fold the omelet such that a third of the omelet is over itself. Push the omelet folded side towards the skillet edge.

8. Gently slide the omelet onto a serving plate ensuring the seam side is down.

9. Repeat the process with the remaining Ingredients then serve and enjoy when hot.

Nutritional Information

- Cal: 576
- Fat: 47.5g
- Carbs: 9.9g
- Fiber: 1.11g
- Protein: 26.3g
- Sugar: 7.2g

Baked Western Omelet

This is an easy, delicious and a perfect lunch omelet dish made of bell peppers, cheese, and ham. This baked western omelet recipe is nice since one can play around with **Ingredients** picking your favorite.

Time: 1 Hour

Servings: 9

Ingredients

- 8 eggs
- 1 cup milk
- Cup green bell pepper (chopped finely)
- tbsp salt (seasoned)
- 8Ounces cooked ham (diced)
- Cup onion (chopped finely)
- Cup cheddar cheese (shredded)
- Cup of red bell pepper (finely chopped)
- Fresh chives

Method

1. Beat the eggs, salt and milk in a mixing bowl then stir in cheese, ham, onion and the bell peppers.

2. Transfer the egg mixture to a baking dish (8-inch-square)

3. Bake for about 45 Minutesto 1 hour at 3500 F until the eggs are well cooked, and the omelet is set.

4. Cut to squares then garnish with chives.

5. Serve and enjoy!!

Nutritional Information

- Calories: 160
- Fat: 10g
- Cholesterol: 168mg
- Sodium: 535mg
- Potassium: 22mg
- Carbs: 3g
- Protein: 13g

Goat Cheese and Fresh Herb Omelet

This is an easy, quick, hearty breakfast omelet with creamy goat cheese. The non-cook cheese best suits those busy mornings. This omelet can served with roasted lemony potatoes.

Time: 15 Minutes

Serving: 1

Ingredients

- 2 tbsp goat cheese (fresh)
- 2 tbsp herbs (freshly chopped)
- 3 eggs
- 2 tbsp whole milk
- tbsp salt
- tbsp black pepper (freshly ground)
- 1 tbsp butter (unsalted)

Method

1. Mash cheese with herbs in a mixing bowl until evenly combined then set aside.

2. In a separate mixing bowl whisk eggs, whole milk, salt, and black pepper until well combined.

3. Heat an eight-inch non-stick skillet over medium-high heat and melt butter until foaming is seen. Stir in the egg mixture until small curds are formed.

4. Shake the skillet gently, so the egg mixture spreads across the skillet. Scoop the cheese gently and pour at the middle third of the cooking egg mixture.

5. Remove skillet from heat and fold the omelet such that a third of the omelet is over itself. Push the omelet folded side towards the skillet edge.

6. Gently slide the omelet onto a serving plate ensuring the seam side is down.

7. Use the remaining herbs for garnish and enjoy.

Nutritional Information

- Cal: 398
- Fat: 32.1g
- Carbs: 1.77g
- Fiber: 0.07g
- Protein: 24.6g
- Sugar: 1.09g

Black Bean Sweet Potato and Egg White Omelet

This is one of the omelet recipes for a busy morning meal. This omelet is incredibly sweet and yummy that you may not require any toppings. It is also super-healthy since sweet potatoes are a rich source of magnesium which helps reduce anxiety and stress.

Time: 12 Minutes

Servings: 1

Ingredients

- 1Cup liquid egg whites
- Fresh cilantro avocado for toppings (optional)
- Cup of sweet potato black bean burrito filling

Method

1. Spray a skillet with cooking spray and heat over high heat.

2. Pour the egg whites to the skillet then add spoonfuls of sweet potato filling over egg whites evenly.

3. Cook for about 5 Minuteson one side until set and bubbly.

4. Flip and cook the other side for another 2 Minutesor until set.

5. Transfer to a plate and top with the cilantro avocado if desired.

6. Enjoy!!

Nutritional Information

- Calories: 249
- Fat: 1.5g
- Sodium: 749.1mg
- Carbs: 26.1g
- Protein: 31g
- Fiber: 5.3g
- Sugar: 3.9g

Pesto Caprese Omelet

This is a quick, easy, and healthy breakfast omelet with fresh pesto, melted mozzarella, and fresh tomatoes bringing out that morning greatness and freshness. It is loved by kids and will leave all members of your family wanting more.

Time: 15 Minutes

Serving: 1

Ingredients

- 1 tomato (ripe and diced)
- 1 tbsp balsamic vinegar
- Salt and pepper
- 2 eggs (lightly beaten)
- 1 tbsp milk
- 1 tbsp pesto
- Salt and pepper
- Cup mozzarella (fresh and torn)
- 1 tbsp pesto

Method

1. Sprinkle tomato in balsamic vinegar, then add salt and pepper for seasoning.

2. Mix eggs, milk, pesto, salt and pepper in a separate bowl.

3. Pour the egg mixture on to a heated non-stick skillet. Swirl the egg mixture to coat.

4. Sprinkle the fresh mozzarella on half the omelet then allow the omelet to cook until the egg set.

5. Sprinkle tomato mixture on half of the omelet. Fold the omelet and enjoy when hot.

Nutritional Information

- Cal: 262
- Fat: 32g
- Carbs: 8g
- Fiber: 1g
- Protein: 26g
- Sugar: 5g

Baked Denver Omelet

This baked Denver omelet is a delicious and easy low carb meal that your family will absolutely love. Ham, being one of the **Ingredients**, contains niacin (b3) which is vital for production of energy and protects one from cancer. Thus, it is a healthy recipe.

Time: 35 Minutes

Servings: 6

Ingredients

- Cup red bell pepper (chopped)
- Cup green bell pepper (chopped)
- Cup yellow onion (chopped)
- 2 tbsp olive oil
- 1 Cup cooked ham (chopped)
- 8 eggs (large)
- Cup milk
- Salt and ground black pepper (freshly)
- Cup sharp cheddar cheese (shredded)
- Sliced avocado (for serving)
- Hot sauce and chopped chives (for serving)

Method

1. Preheat an oven to 4000 F then spray a medium baking dish with cooking spray.

2. Evenly sprinkle ham to the baking dish bottom.

3. Over high heat, heat olive oil in a skillet then add green bell peppers, red bell peppers, and onions. Cook for about 4 Minutesor until softened.

4. Pour the pepper mixture over ham layer then top with cheese.

5. Mix eggs and milk in a mixing bowl until completely blended. Season with pepper and salt then stir. Pour the mixture in the baking dish.

6. Bake for about 25 Minutesin the oven until puffy.

7. Cut into 6 pieces and serve with avocado, hot sauce, and chives.

8. Enjoy!

Nutritional Information

- Calories: 212
- Fat: 14g
- Cholesterol: 250mg
- Sodium: 198mg
- Potassium: 169mg
- Carbs: 3g
- Protein: 16g
- Sugar: 2g

Bacon Cheeseburger Omelet

This is dish delivers delicious bacon cheeseburger flavors wrapped in an omelet making it hearty and perfect bacon and egg combination. This cheeseburger is the best choice for your breakfast.

Time: 30 Minutes

Serving: 4

Ingredients

For Burger

- 6 strips bacon
- 1 onion (diced)
- 1 garlic clove (chopped)
- 1 pound beef (ground)
- cup ketchup
- 1 tbsp Worcestershire sauce
- 1 tbsp yellow mustard
- Salt and pepper

For Omelet

- 8 eggs
- Cup cream or milk
- Salt and pepper
- Cup lettuce
- Cup tomato (diced)
- Cup onion (sliced)
- Cup pickle (diced)
- Cup cheddar cheese (shredded)

Method

For Burger

1. Cook the bacon strips in a skillet then place on paper towels to crumble and drain the cooking grease.

2. Add the diced onions to the skillet and cook over medium heat until tender.

3. Add chopped garlic and continue cooking until fragrant. Add beef and cook while draining any grease.

4. Stir in ketchup, Worcestershire sauce, yellow mustard, salt, and pepper. Simmer then set aside.

For Omelet

5. Whisk eggs and milk together then season with pepper and salt.

6. Heat your skillet over medium-high heat. Pour a quarter of the egg mixture onto then skillet ensuring the base of the pan is coated. Cook until the egg set.

7. Sprinkle a quarter cooked beef, lettuce, diced tomato, sliced onion, and diced pickle onto half side of the omelet. Cover by folding the other omelet half over.

8. Sprinkle cheddar cheese then cover and cook until cheese melts.

9. Repeat the process with the rest of the Ingredients.

10. Enjoy.

Nutritional Information

- Cal: 456
- Fat: 21.4g
- Carbs: 10g
- Fiber: 1.2g
- Protein: 54g
- Sugar: 7g

Bacon Spinach Omelet

Bacon spinach omelet is a very easy dish to make. It is a super healthy recipe as bacon is a good source of the omega-3's that helps reduce cholesterol in your body and improve overall heart health.

Time: 10 Minutes

Servings: 1

Ingredients

- 4 beaten eggs
- 3 tbsp milk
- Pepper and salt to taste
- Cup chopped spinach
- Cups sliced cherry tomatoes
- 4 cut and cooked bacon slices
- Cup grated cheese

Method

1. Preheat an oven to 4500 F. Meanwhile, beat eggs in a bowl. Add milk, pepper, and salt the beat again.

2. Grease a pan and heat over high heat then pour the egg mixture and cook for about 2 Minutesuntil eggs are well-cooked.

3. Add tomatoes, spinach, cheese, and bacon. Place in the oven.

4. Cook for about 2 Minutesuntil eggs are cooked on top.

5. Remove from oven and close the sides over.

6. Top with any remainder from the INGREDIENTS

7. Enjoy!!

Nutritional Information

- Calories: 883
- Fat: 71g
- Cholesterol: 776mg
- Sodium: 1218mg
- Potassium: 696mg
- Carbs: 7g
- Protein: 49g
- Sugar: 4g

Mushroom and Fine Herbs Omelet

These are awesomely delicious mushroom omelets full flavors and nutrients to kick off your day. These omelets can be taken for breakfast, lunch, and dinner. Use more herbs for garnishing and enhanced flavors.

Time: 45 Minutes

Serving: 4

Ingredients

- 1 pound baby Portobello mushrooms (sliced)
- 2 tbsp butter
- Cup white wine
- 1 tbsp each parsley, tarragon, and chives (fresh and minced)
- tbsp chervil (dried)
- tbsp salt
- tbsp pepper

Asiago Sauce

- 2 tbsp butter
- 2 tbsp all-purpose flour
- 1 cup milk
- Cup Asiago cheese
- tbsp salt

Omelet

- 4 tbsp butter (divided)
- 8 eggs
- cup water
- More herbs (fresh and minced)

Method

1. Heat butter in a non-stick skillet then cook mushrooms until tender. Stir in wine followed by herbs, salt, and pepper.

2. In another pan heat butter then add all-purpose flour while stirring and gradually adding milk. Cook until the mixture is thick then add Asiago cheese and salt. Ensure it stays warm.

3. In another skillet heat a tbsp of butter. Meanwhile, whisk in eggs and water until well combined. Pour two third of the egg mixture to the skillet and cook until set.

4. Scoop a half cup of mushroom mixture and pour on one half of the egg. Fold the other half to cover the filling.

5. Carefully place the omelet on a serving place then top with a quarter cup sauce.

6. Repeat with the rest of the INGREDIENTS to make three more omelets.

Nutritional Information

- Cal: 388
- Fat: 29g
- Carbs: 12g
- Fiber: 2g
- Protein: 20g
- Sugar: 6g

Big Steak Omelet

This is a delicious, heavy breakfast omelet meal enough to be a dinner. Steak is a rich source of L-carnitine which plays an important role in transporting fats to mitochondria for burning.

Time: 40 Minutes

Servings: 2

Ingredients

- 4 beaten eggs
- Pepper and salt to taste
- Lb flank steak
- tbsp butter
- 1cup shredded hash browns
- tbsp cayenne
- tbsp paprika
- diced green pepper
- diced sweet onion
- 4Oz sliced Portobello mushrooms
- 1cup shredded cheddar cheese
- 1 diced plum tomato

Method

1. Season the steak and grill to medium then let cool and slice.

2. Over high heat, melt butter in a pan then add hash browns. Add pepper, salt, paprika, and cayenne then stir and cook for about 5 minutes. Remove from pan and set aside

3. Sauté mushrooms in the same pan for about 2 Minutesuntil cooked. Remove from pan and set aside.

4. Season the eggs with pepper and salt then stir in sweet onions and green peppers.

5. Grease a skillet over medium heat and pour the egg mixture in. Cook until edges and bottom are solid.

6. Add two-thirds steak, hash browns cup cheddar cheese, two-thirds tomatoes, and two-thirds mushrooms to half of the omelet and fold.

7. Continue to cook until cheese melts.

8. Top with any leftovers from the INGREDIENTS and serve.

9. Enjoy!

Nutritional Information

- Calories: 843
- Fat: 49.8g
- Cholesterol: 457mg
- Sodium: 839mg
- Potassium: 1340mg
- Carbs: 36.5g
- Protein: 61.4g

Herbs Omelet

These thin herbs omelets are delicious, rich in nutrients and best suited those busy mornings. They can be prepared overnight or ahead of time then warmed in the morning for breakfast. The omelets can also be taken as a light lunch or as a snack.

Time: 25 Minutes

Serving: 4

Ingredients

- 5 eggs
- Cup whole milk
- Cup herbs (finely chopped)
- Salt
- Black pepper
- 4 tbsp vegetable oil
- sour sauce

Method

1. Preheat your oven to 3000 F then arrange the rack at the middle.

2. Whisk together eggs, whole milk, salt, and pepper until eggs break up.

3. Heat a non-stick skillet over medium heat then melt vegetable oil until it shimmers. Pour a third of a cup of your egg mixture onto the skillet and spread it into a thin layer.

4. Cook until the edges are slightly brown for about thirty seconds.

5. Slide the omelet on a baking sheet.

6. Prepare three more omelets with the remained egg mixture stalking them on the baking sheet.

7. Apply quarter sour sauce on a half omelet then fold into half to cover the sour sauce. Fold again to form a fan shape then place on your baking sheet.

8. Repeat the process with the remained sour sauce. Heat on the oven and serve when hot.

Nutritional Information

- Cal: 195
- Fat: 15.23g
- Carbs: 5g
- Fiber: 0.73g
- Protein: 10.2g
- Sugar: 1.6g

Fresh Corn Omelet

This is one of the easiest omelet recipes to make. It is a super-healthy recipe as corn is a decent source of phosphorus which is a mineral that plays an important role in maintenance and growth of body tissues.

Time: 25 Minutes

Servings: 4

Ingredients

- 10 eggs (large)
- 2 tbsp water
- tbsp salt
- tbsp pepper
- 2, 2 tbsp butter
- 1 cup fresh corn
- cup cheddar cheese (shredded)
- Fresh salsa

Method

1. Whisk eggs, pepper, salt, and water in a mixing bowl until blended. Set aside.

2. Over high heat, heat 2tsp butter in a skillet then add corn. Cook for about 2 Minuteswhile stirring until tender. Set aside.

3. Heat 1tsp butter in the same pan and pour in the half of the egg mixture. Cook until eggs are well cooked, and the omelet is almost set.

4. Spoon half the corn and 0.25cup cheese on half of the omelet. Fold and cut into half. Place each half to a plate.

5. Repeat for the remaining butter, filling and the egg mixture.

6. Serve with salsa.

Nutritional Information

- Calories: 336
- Fat: 25g
- Cholesterol: 500mg
- Sodium: 482mg
- Carbs: 8g
- Sugar: 3g
- Fiber: 1g
- Protein: 20g

Conclusion

It's no secret; an omelet delivers a plethora of health benefits. In addition, these meals are easy to make and can be incorporated into any meal plan with ease. However, due to their simplicity, the dishes can make you want to take them every morning, and this can be risky.

To get optimal benefits, you must take omelets regularly, and in the right amounts. Too much of omelet, taken too often can result in problems such as increased fat and cholesterol levels, protein allergy, the risk of cardiovascular diseases, and risk of type 2 diabetes. As a parent, it's your role to ensure toddlers take limited amounts of the omelet as they are most susceptible to protein allergy.

Author's Afterthoughts

Thanks ever so much to each of my cherished readers for investing the time to read this book!

I know you could have picked from many other books but you chose this one. So a big thanks for downloading this book and reading all the way to the end.

If you enjoyed this book or received value from it, I'd like to ask you for a favor. Please take a few Minutesto post an honest and heartfelt review on Amazon.com. Your support does make a difference and helps to benefit other people.

Thanks!

Daniel Humphreys

About the Author

Daniel Humphreys

Many people will ask me if I am German or Norman, and my answer is that I am 100% unique! Joking aside, I owe my cooking influence mainly to my mother who was British! I can certainly make a mean Sheppard's pie, but when it comes to preparing Bratwurst sausages and drinking beer with friends, I am also all in!

I am taking you on this culinary journey with me and hope you can appreciate my diversified background. In my 15 years career as a chef, I never had a dish returned to me by one of clients, so that should say something about me! Actually, I will take that back. My worst critic is my four years old son, who refuses to taste anything that is green color. That shall pass, I am sure.

My hope is to help my children discover the joy of cooking and sharing their creations with their loved ones, like I did all my life. When you develop a passion for cooking and my suspicious is that you have one as well, it usually sticks for life. The best advice I can give anyone as a professional chef is invest. Invest your time, your heart in each meal you are creating. Invest also a little money in good cooking hardware and quality ingredients. But most of all enjoy every meal you prepare with YOUR friends and family!

Made in the USA
Monee, IL
22 August 2021